The Family at Church

FAMILY GUIDANCE SERIES

By Joel R. Beeke

The church must maintain the divinely ordered role of the family to establish a godly heritage. In this ongoing series, Dr. Joel R. Beeke offers pastoral insight and biblical direction for building strong Christian families.

Books in the series:
Bringing the Gospel to Covenant Children
A Loving Encouragement to Flee Worldliness
Family Worship
The Family at Church

The Family at Church
Listening to Sermons and Attending Prayer Meetings

Joel R. Beeke

REFORMATION HERITAGE BOOKS
Grand Rapids, Michigan

The Family at Church
© 2004, 2008 by Joel R. Beeke

Reformation Heritage Books
3070 29th St. SE
Grand Rapids, MI 49512
616-977-0599
e-mail: orders@heritagebooks.org
website: www.heritagebooks.org

Printed in the United States of America
21 22 23 24 25 26/11 10 9 8 7 6 5 4

Library of Congress Cataloging-in-Publication Data

Beeke, Joel R., 1952-
  The family at church : listening to sermons and attending
prayer meetings / Joel R. Beeke. — 2nd ed.
      p. cm.
  Includes index.
  ISBN 978-1-60178-043-0 (pbk. : alk. paper)
 1. Prayer meetings. 2. Family—Religious life. 3. Worship
(Religious
education) 4. Preaching. 5. Public worship. 6. Church atten-
dance. I.
Title.
  BV285.B35 2008
  264'.7—dc22

                          2008027886

*For additional Reformed literature, both new and used,
request a free book list from the above address.*

For

Henry and Lena Kamp

the world's best in-laws
godly, gracious, giving, and grateful

CONTENTS

Listening to Sermons

Attending Prayer Meetings

Listening to Sermons

"Take heed therefore how ye hear."
— Luke 8:18

The Importance of Preaching

John Calvin often instructed his congregation about rightly hearing the Word of God. He taught them how they should come to public worship and how to hear the Word of God preached. Calvin wanted parents and children to grasp the importance of preaching, to desire preaching as a supreme blessing, and to participate actively in the sermon. Calvin said listeners should have the "willingness to obey God completely and with no reserve."[1]

Calvin stressed listening to the preached Word for two important reasons. First, he believed that few people listen well to sermons. More than thirty times in his commentaries and nine times in his *Institutes*, Calvin referred to how few people receive the preached Word with saving faith. He said, "If the same sermon is preached, say, to a hundred people, twenty receive it with the ready obedience of faith,

---

1. Leroy Nixon, *John Calvin, Expository Preacher* (Grand Rapids: Eerdmans, 1950), 65.

while the rest hold it valueless, or laugh, or hiss, or loathe it."[2] If proper hearing was a problem in Calvin's day, how much more is it so today, when ministers have to compete for the attention of people who are bombarded with various forms of media on a daily basis?

Second, Calvin stressed proper hearing because of his high regard for preaching. Calvin viewed preaching as a means God used to bestow salvation and benediction. Calvin said the Holy Spirit is the 'internal minister' who uses the 'external minister' of the preached Word. The external minister "holds forth the vocal word and it is received by the ears," but the internal minister "truly communicates the thing proclaimed, [which] is Christ."[3] Thus, God speaks through the mouth of His servants by His Spirit: "Wherever the gospel is preached, it is as if God himself came into the midst of us."[4] Faithful preaching is the means by which the Spirit does His saving work of illuminating, converting, and sealing sinners. Calvin said, "There is...an inward efficacy of the Holy Spirit when

2. John Calvin, *Institutes of the Christian Religion*, ed. John T. McNeill, trans. Ford Lewis Battles (Philadelphia: Westminster Press, 1960), 3.24.12.

3. John Calvin, *Tracts and Treatises*, trans. Henry Beveridge (Grand Rapids: Eerdmans, 1958), 1:173.

4. John Calvin, *Commentary* on the Synoptic Gospels (Edinburgh: Calvin Translation Society, 1851), 3:129.

he sheds forth his power upon hearers, that they may embrace a discourse [sermon] by faith."[5]

Like Calvin, the Puritans had a high regard for preaching. As lovers of the Word of God, the Puritans were not content with merely affirming the infallibility, inerrancy, and authority of Scripture. They also read, searched, preached, heard, and sang the Word with delight, seeking the applying power of the Holy Spirit that accompanied the Word. They regarded the sixty-six books of Holy Scripture as the library of the Holy Spirit. For the Puritans, Scripture was God speaking to His people as a father speaks to his children. In preaching, God gives His Word as truth and power. As truth, Scripture can be trusted for time and eternity. As power, Scripture is the instrument of transformation used by the Spirit of God to renew our minds.

As twenty-first-century evangelical Protestants, we must combine our defense of biblical inerrancy with a positive demonstration of the transforming power of God's Word. That power must be manifest in our lives, our homes, our churches, and our communities. We must show that, though other books may inform or even reform us, only one Book can transform us, conforming us to the image of Christ. Only as "living epistles of Christ" (2 Cor. 3:3) can we hope to win the battle for the Bible in our day. If we spent most of our energy on knowing and living the

---

5. *Commentary* on Ezekiel, 1:61.

Scriptures, how many more people would fall under the sway of its transforming power?

The Puritan movement teaches us much about cultivating the transforming power of the Word. Puritan preachers clearly explained how the Word effected personal transformation. They offered practical direction on how to read and listen to God's Word.[6] The Westminster Larger Catechism summarizes such Puritan advice in Question 160: "It is

---

6. Samuel Annesley, "How May We Give Christ a Satisfying Account [of] Why we Attend upon the Ministry of the Word?," in *Puritan Sermons 1659-1689, Being Morning Exercises at Cripplegate* (Wheaton, Ill.: Richard Owen Roberts, 1981), 4:173–98; David Clarkson, "Hearing the Word," *The Works of David Clarkson* (Edinburgh: Banner of Truth Trust, 1988), 1:428–46; Thomas Manton, "The Life of Faith in Hearing the Word," *The Complete Works of Thomas Manton* (London: James Nisbet, 1873), 15:154–74; Jonathan Edwards, "Profitable Hearers of the Word," *The Works of Jonathan Edwards: Sermons and Discourses 1723–1729,* ed. Kenneth P. Minkema (New Haven: Yale, 1997), 14:243–77; Thomas Senior, "How We May Hear the Word with Profit," in *Puritan Sermons*, 2:47–57; Thomas Watson on hearing the Word effectually, *A Body of Divinity* (Grand Rapids: Sovereign Grace Publishers, 1972), 377–80; three short pieces by Thomas Boston, *The Complete Works of the Late Rev. Thomas Boston* (Wheaton, Ill.: Richard Owen Roberts, 1980), 2:427–54; Thomas Shepard's "Of Ineffectual Hearing the Word," *The Works of Thomas Shepard* (Ligonier, Penn.: Soli Deo Gloria, 1992), 3:363–84.

Several nineteenth-century sources stand in the Puritan tradition: a letter by John Newton entitled "Hearing Sermons," *The Works of John Newton* (Edinburgh: Banner of Truth Trust, 1985), 1:218–25; an essay by John Elias entitled "On hearing the Gospel," *John Elias: Life, Letters and Essays* (Edinburgh: Banner of Truth Trust, 1973), 356–60; and the most thorough and helpful

required of those that hear the word preached, that they attend upon it with diligence, preparation, and prayer, examine what they hear by the Scriptures, receive the truth with faith, love, meekness, and readiness of mind, as the word of God; meditate, and confer of it in their hearts, and bring forth the fruit of it in their lives."[7]

In conjunction with Luke 8:18, "Take heed therefore how ye hear," I will offer some Puritan teachings along with my own observations on listening to God's Word, dividing the subject into three thoughts: how to prepare for the preached Word, how to receive the preached Word, and how to practice the preached Word. While studying each point, we should ask ourselves: Am I really hearing the Word of God? Am I a good listener of the proclaimed gospel, or am I only a critical or careless hearer? Do I realize, as Charles Simeon said, that every sermon "increases either our salvation or condemnation"?[8] Am I teaching my children how to be good listeners?

---

treatment, Edward Bickersteth, *The Christian Hearer* (London: Seeleys, 1853).

7. *Westminster Confession of Faith* (Glasgow: Free Presbyterian Publications, 1997), 253.

8. Charles Simeon, *Let Wisdom Judge: University Addresses and Sermon Outlines* (Nottingham: Inter-Varsity Fellowship, 1959), 19.

Preparing for the Preached Word 2

"It is required of those that hear the word preached, that they attend upon it with diligence, preparation, and prayer," the Westminster divines wrote (*LC*, Q. 160). This involves several, practical applications:

1. Before coming to God's house to hear His Word, prepare yourself and your family *with prayer*. The Puritans said we should dress our bodies for worship and our souls with prayer.

Pray for the conversion of sinners, the edification of saints, and the glorification of God's triune name. Pray for children, teenagers, and the elderly. Pray for listening ears and understanding hearts. Pray for yourself, saying: "Lord, how real the danger is that I will not hear well! Of four kinds of hearers in the parable of the sower, only one kind heard properly. Help me, Lord, to concentrate fully on Thy Word as it comes to me, so that I may not hear the Word and yet perish. Let Thy Word have free course in my heart. Let it be accompanied with light, power, and grace."

Pray that you will come to God's house as a needy

sinner, purging your heart of carnal lusts and cling-
ing to Christ for the cleansing power of His blood.
Pray for the sanctifying presence of God in Christ, for
true communion with Him in mind and soul.

Pray that your minister will receive the unction of
the Holy Spirit, so that he will open his mouth boldly
to make known the mysteries of the gospel (cf. Eph.
6:19). Pray for an outpouring of the Spirit's convict-
ing, quickening, humbling, and comforting power to
work through God's ordinances in the fulfillment of
His promises (Prov. 1:23).

2. Come with a *hearty appetite* for the Word. A good
appetite promotes good digestion and growth. Peter
encouraged spiritual appetite, saying, "As newborn
babes, desire the sincere milk of the word, that ye
may grow thereby" (1 Pet. 2:2). Likewise, Solomon
advised, "Keep thy foot when thou goest to the house
of God, and be more ready to hear, than to offer the
sacrifice of fools" (Eccles. 5:1).

A good appetite for the Word means having a tender, teachable heart (2 Chron. 13:7) that asks, "Lord,
what wilt thou have me to do?" (Acts 9:6). It is fool-
ish to expect a blessing if you come to worship with a
hardened, unprepared, or worldly-minded heart.[1]

The Puritans said preparation for worship should
start on Saturday evening. Just as people baked
bread on Saturday evening so it would be warm on

---

1. Watson, *Body of Divinity*, 377.

Sunday morning, so people should study the Word on Saturday evenings so that their hearts would be warm for worship on Sunday.

If you know the passage that will be preached on the Sabbath, spend time studying it on Saturday night. Make sure that you and your children get enough sleep on Saturday night, then get up early on Sunday morning to prepare for worship without rushing.

3. Meditate on *the importance of the preached Word* as you enter God's house. The high and holy triune God of heaven and earth is meeting with you to speak directly to you. Thomas Boston wrote, "The voice is on earth, [but] the speaker is in heaven" (Acts 10:33).[2] What an awe-inspiring thought! Since the gospel is the Word of God, not the word of man, come to church looking for God. Though you should deeply appreciate your minister's efforts to faithfully bring you the Word of God, pray that you see "no man, save Jesus only" (Matt. 17:8). Ministers are simply God's ambassadors, bringing you the Word of God (2 Cor. 5:20; Heb. 13:7). Do not focus on them but on the Word of God they bring, always remembering that one day you will give an account before God of every sermon that He has brought to you.

Teach your children that every sermon counts for eternity. Salvation comes through faith, and faith comes through hearing God's Word (Rom. 10:13–16).

---

2. Boston, *Works*, 2:28.

So every sermon is a matter of life and death (Deut. 32:47; 2 Cor. 2:15–16). The preached gospel will either lift us up to heaven or cast us down to hell. It will advance our salvation or aggravate our condemnation. It will draw us with the cords of love or leave us in the snares of unbelief. It will soften or harden us (Matt. 13:14–15), enlighten or darken our eyes (Rom. 11:10), open our heart to Christ or shut it against Him. "The nearer to heaven any are lifted up by gospel preaching, the lower will they sink into hell if they heed it not," wrote David Clarkson.[3] "Take heed, therefore, how ye hear!"

Furthermore, remember that every Sabbath you are receiving spiritual food and supplies for the coming week. The Puritans called the Sabbath "the market day of the soul."[4] As the Puritans went to market each week to stock up on supplies, so we stock up on our spiritual goods for the week by listening to sermons, then meditating on them throughout the week to come. All of that must be reinforced with daily devotions and Christian living.

4. Remember as you enter the house of God that *you are entering a battleground*. Many enemies will oppose your listening. Internally, you may be distracted by worldly cares and employments, lusts of

---

3. Clarkson, *Works*, 1:430–31.

4. See James T. Dennison, Jr., *The Market Day of the Soul: The Puritan Doctrine of the Sabbath in England, 1532–1700* (Grand Rapids: Reformation Heritage Books, 2008).

the flesh, cold hearts, and critical spirits. Externally, you may be distracted by the temperature or weather, behavior or dress of others, noises, or people moving about. Satan opposes your listening to God's Word with might and main, knowing that if you truly hear it, he will lose you. So Satan tries to disturb you before the sermon begins, distracts you during the sermon, and dismisses the sermon from your mind as soon as it is finished. Like a bird plucking away newly sown seed, Satan attempts to snatch the Word from your mind and heart so that it cannot take root. When you are tempted during worship by Satan, Samuel Annesley advises that you rebuke him, saying, "Be gone, Satan! I will parley no longer. If others neglect salvation, therefore must I? Will their missing of salvation relieve me for the loss of mine? Through Christ, I defy you."[5] Pray repeatedly for strength to overcome all your enemies by listening well.

5. Finally, come with *a loving, expectant faith* (Ps. 62:1, 5). Be swift to hear, slow to speak, and determined, like Mary, to ponder God's Word in your heart. Come pleading God's promise that His Word will not return to Him void (Isa. 55:10–11). Come with the spirit of the Ninevites, saying, "Who can tell if God will turn and repent, and turn away from his fierce anger, that we perish not?" (Jonah 3:9).

Come with reverential fear of God and His majesty.

---

5. *Puritan Sermons,* 4:187.

Come with reverential delight in God and His Word (Ps. 119:97, 103). Say like David in Psalm 119:140, "Thy word is very pure; therefore thy servant loveth it." Like David, love God's testimonies "exceedingly" (v. 167), more than gold (v. 127), to the point where it nearly consumes you (v. 20). David's love for God's Word was so fervent that he would meditate upon it "all the day" (v. 97). In dependence on the Spirit, cultivate such love for the Word of God.

Receiving the Preached Word | 3 |

King James II of England, when battling the Puritans, sent a proclamation to all the ministers in the Church of England, demanding that it be read to every congregation on Sunday. Knowing that the bill opposed New Testament Christianity as well as the Puritan style of preaching, the Puritans detested reading this enactment. One Puritan preacher responded by saying to his congregation, "I must read this bill from King James II in this church building, but it does not say that you have to listen to it." The congregation left the church, and the minister read the bill to an empty church. The point of the story is this: many people listen halfheartedly to sermons, as if they were not compelled to hear the Word of God; likewise, many preachers preach as if they were addressing empty pews instead of people with eternal souls.

The Word of God must engage both the minister and the listener. Growth cannot take place if the listener does not profit from the Word. That reception involves, as the Westminster divines put it, that

"those that hear the word preached [should] examine what they hear by the Scriptures, [and] receive
the truth with faith, love, meekness, and readiness
of mind, as the word of God" (*LC*, Q. 160). Here are
some guidelines for listening rightly to God's Word.

1. Listen with *an understanding, tender conscience.*
Jesus' parable of the sower (Matt. 13:3–23; Mark
4:1–20; Luke 8:4–15) presents us with four types of
listeners, all of whom hear the same word:

- The stony-hearted, superficial listener. This
  listener is like a hard path. The sower's seed,
  or the Word of God, makes little impres-
  sion on this hard heart. The gospel does not
  penetrate this listener, and the law does not
  frighten him. A minister could preach through
  all the Ten Commandments, addressing the
  needs and sins of the people, but the stony
  listener shrugs it off. If a minister addresses
  this person's conscience, this hardened heart
  shifts the blame to others. He seldom changes
  his life because of conviction from the Word of
  God. He does not take preaching to heart.

- The easily impressed but resistant listener.
  Some seed falls on rocky ground. A plant
  begins to spring up from this seed, but it soon
  withers and dies because it lacks sufficient
  nutrients. The plant cannot survive because
  it cannot grow roots among the rocks. Jesus
  presents here a listener that seems initially to
  listen well to the Word. This listener would like

to add religion to his life, but he does not want to hear about the kind of radical discipleship that involves self-denial, taking up his cross, and following Christ. Thus, when persecution comes, this listener fails to live out the gospel in practical ways. He wants to be friends with the world, the church, and with God. Like Israel, this listener does not respond to God's Word when challenged to choose: "How long halt ye between two opinions? If the LORD be God, follow him: but if Baal, then follow him. And the people answered him not a word" (1 Kings 18:21). As listeners, we cannot have God and the world; friendship with the world is enmity against God. We must make a choice.

• The half-hearted, distracted listener. Some of the seed of God's Word falls in thorn-ridden soil. As Luke 8:14 says, "And that which fell among thorns are they, which, when they have heard, go forth, and are choked with cares and riches and pleasures of this life, and bring no fruit to perfection." This kind of listener tries to absorb the Word of God with one ear while thinking with the other about business, interest rates, pension funds, and inflation. He only serves God partially. The Word of God is quickly choked by the thorns.

• The understanding, fruitful listener. Some of God's seed falls on rich, fertile soil. Jesus says this listener hears and understands God's Word (Matt. 13:23). Just as a seed quickly takes root in fertile soil, so the truth of God

implants itself into this listener's eager heart.
As a plant springs up, growing deep roots and
showing healthy leaves, the Word of God is
deeply integrated into this listener's life, family, business, relationships, and conduct. With
the help of the Holy Spirit, this listener applies
the gospel teaching he hears on Sunday to his
life throughout the week. He believes with
his heart that if Jesus Christ has sacrificed
everything for him, nothing is too difficult
to surrender in grateful obedience to Christ.
Before all else, he seeks the kingdom of God
(Matt. 6:33). Grace reigns in his heart. He
brings forth fruit, "some an hundredfold, some
sixty, some thirty" (Matt. 13:23).

2. Listen *attentively* to the preached Word. Luke
19:48 describes people who were very attentive to
Christ. Literally translated, the text says, "they hung
upon him, hearing." Lydia showed such an open heart
when she "attended" or "turned her mind" to the
things spoken by Paul (Acts 16:14). Such attentive-
ness involves banishing wandering thoughts, dullness
of mind, and drowsiness (Matt. 13:25). It regards a
sermon as a matter of life and death (Deut. 32:47).

We must not listen to sermons as spectators but
as participants. The minister should not be the only
one working. Good listening is hard work; it involves
worshiping God continuously. An attentive listener
responds quickly — whether with repentance, resolu-
tion, determination, or praise — and God is honored
in this. As Proverbs 18:15 says, "The heart of the

prudent getteth knowledge; and the ear of the wise seeketh knowledge." The verbs used here refer to energetic, mental action.

Too many people come to church expecting to be spoon-fed. They have no desire to think or learn or grow. They simply want to hear familiar preaching. They are not anxious to grow in the grace and knowledge of the Lord Jesus Christ. Such passivity seems abnormal, since in other areas of life, humans resist being spoon-fed. A child would be embarrassed if his mother fed him in front of friends. In school and at work, people expect intellectual challenges. Yet at church, some people do not want to be challenged emotionally, intellectually, or spiritually. They would rather be patted on the back or left alone than be convicted and challenged by God's Word. Instead of hearing clear instruction on Christian living from Paul's epistles, such people would rather hear little more than a Bible story every Sunday.

Jesus did not spoon-feed His hearers. In one parable, Jesus talked about an unjust judge. Jesus compared God to this judge, but He did not waste time with a lengthy explanation of how God is not unjust. Rather, Jesus challenged His hearers to use their minds to work through the difficult teaching of this parable. Because He expected His listeners to be discerning and assertive, Jesus could make strong statements without apology. For example, in Luke 14:26, Jesus said, "If any man come to me, and hate not his father, and mother, and wife, and children, and brethren, and sisters, yea, and his own life also, he cannot be my disciple." Jesus often let the truth He proclaimed stand alone, without explanation. For example, He spoke about cutting off hands, plucking out eyes, and cutting off feet. He said some of the children of darkness are smarter than the children of light. He used metaphors, hyperbole, and other figures of speech. Running the risk of being misunderstood, He refused to spoon-feed those who were following Him.

Jesus told His listeners, "Take heed therefore how you hear." He also commanded us to understand what we hear. He challenges us to *think*, and that takes work. The word *attend* is derived from two Latin words—the first means 'to' and the second, 'tendo,' which means 'to stretch or bend.' From this we get the word *tendon*, or a sinew that stretches. Thus, the word *attend* literally means we must stretch our minds by listening. This implies reaching out with all our mental and spiritual powers to grasp the meaning of a message. Are you stretching your spiritual muscles as you listen to the Word? Are you *attentive* to the preached Word?

As you listen to the Word of God, ask yourself, *how does God want me to be different on account of this sermon?* Ask what God wants you to know that you did not know before. Ask what truths you are learning that He wants you to believe. And ask how He wants you to put those truths into practice. In every sermon you hear—even those on the most basic gospel themes — God offers you truths to believe and put into practice. Pray for grace to work at listening.

3. Listen with *submissive faith*. As James 1:21 says, "Receive with meekness the engrafted word." This kind of meekness involves a submissive frame of heart, "a willingness to hear the counsels and reproofs of the word."[1] Through this kind of faith, the Word is engrafted into the soul and produces "the sweet fruit of righteousness."[2]

Faith is the key to profitably receiving the Word. Luther wrote, "Faith is not an achievement, it is a gift. Yet it comes only through the hearing and study of the Word." If the chief ingredient of a medicine is missing, the medicine will not be effective. So be sure not to leave out the chief ingredient, faith, as you listen to a sermon. Seek grace to believe and apply the whole Word (Rom. 13:14), along with the promises, the invitations, and the admonitions as they are spoken.[3]

"The whole Word is the object of faith," wrote Thomas Manton. Therefore we need "faith in the histories, for our warning and caution; faith in the doctrines, to increase our reverence and admiration; faith in the threatenings, for our humiliation; faith in the precepts, for our subjection; and faith in the

---

1. Watson, *Body of Divinity*, 377.

2. Ibid., 378.

3. Ibid.

promises, for our consolation. They all have their use: the histories to make us wary and cautious; the doctrines to enlighten us with a true sense of God's nature and will; the precepts to direct us, and to try and regulate our obedience; the promises to cheer and comfort us; the threatenings to terrify us, to run anew to Christ, to bless God for our escape, and to add spurs to our duty."[4]

4. Listen with *humility and serious self-examination*. Do I humbly examine myself under the preaching of God's Word, trembling at its impact (Isa. 66:2)? Do I cultivate a meek and submissive spirit, receiving God's truth as a student while being intimately aware of my own depravity? Do I seriously examine myself under preaching, listening for my own instruction rather than for the instruction of others? We must not respond like Peter, who said to Jesus, "Lord, and what shall this man do?" We must listen to Jesus' admonition: "What is that to thee? follow thou me" (John 21:21–22). When the marks of grace are set before us, we must ask: Do I experience these marks? Do I listen for the truths of God, wanting to be admonished or corrected where I have gone astray? Do I relish having the Word of God applied to my life? Do I pray

---

4. Thomas Manton, *The Life of Faith* (Ross-shire, Scotland: Christian Focus, 1997), 223–24.

that the Spirit may apply His Word, as Robert Burns put it, to my "business and bosom"?[5]

When a doctor tells you how to maintain your health or that of your children, do you not listen carefully so that you can follow his directions? When the heavenly Physician gives you divine directions for your soul, should you not listen every bit as carefully so that you can follow God's instructions for your life?

5. *The Works of Thomas Halyburton* (London: Thomas Tegg, 1835), xiv.

Practicing the Preached Word $\boxed{4}$

The Westminster divines said that "it is required of those that hear the word preached, that they…meditate, and confer of it in their hearts, and bring forth the fruit of it in their lives" (*LC*, Q. 160). Thus the Word attended must also be practiced. Here are some ways.

1. *Strive to retain and pray over what you have heard.* Hebrews 2:1 says, "We ought to give earnest heed to the things which we have heard, lest at any time we should let them slip." Thomas Watson said we should not let sermons run through our minds like water through a sieve. "Our memories should be like the chest of the ark, where the law was put," he wrote.[1] Joseph Alleine said one way to remember the preached Word is to "come from your knees to the sermon, and come from the sermon to your knees."[2]

---

1. Watson, *Body of Divinity*, 378.

2. Joseph Alleine, *A Sure Guide to Heaven* (Edinburgh: Banner of Truth Trust, 1999), 29.

Many people find note-taking helpful in retaining the teaching of a sermon. An elderly woman told me, "I take thorough sermon notes. When I bow my knees on Sunday evening, I put my notes in front of me, underline those things that I should strive to put into practice, and then pray through them one at a time." For many people taking notes helps them remember specific ways in which God challenges their hearts. Recognize, however, that note-taking is not for everyone. For some people, writing gets in the way of active listening, because it makes them lose their train of thought. In that case, note-taking does more harm than good. Do whatever helps you remember and pray over the sermons you hear.

2. *Familiarize yourself with the truths you have heard.* The Westminster Directory for Public Worship advises parents to engage in "repetition of sermons, especially by calling their families to an account of what they have heard."[3] When you come home from church, speak to your loved ones about the sermon you have heard in an edifying, practical manner. Talk about the sermon in words that your youngest child will understand.

Encourage your children to take notes on the sermon. My wife and I have trained our children since they were age seven to take notes. After the last service each Sabbath, we read through those notes as a

---

3. *Westminster Confession of Faith*, 386.

family and talk our way through the sermons. Some-times the discussions help our children more than the sermons themselves. Even when conversation does not produce the desired results, continue to attempt this review of Sabbath sermons. It is better to fall short than not to attempt at all.

In addition, speak with fellow believers about the sermons. God's blessing rests upon such fellowship. Malachi 3:16 says, "Then they that feared the LORD spake often one to another: and the LORD hearkened, and heard it, and a book of remembrance was writ-ten before him for them that feared the LORD, and that thought upon his name."

Share some of the lessons you are learning from the Word. As you talk with others, these lessons will help others as well as become more embedded in your own mind. Proverbs 27:17 says, "Iron sharp-eneth iron; so a man sharpeneth the countenance of his friend."

Do not engage in frivolous, worldly conversation after a sermon. Shallow talk about politics, people, sports, or news events is Satan's way of sending his vultures to pluck away the good seed of the Word. Instead, talk about the Bible, Christ, the soul, and the eternal world as it applies to the sermon. And when you talk about the sermon, avoid a critical spirit. Do not judge the sermon harshly. Such a spirit dampens spiritual life. Do not talk about what was missing, but concentrate on what was said. Listen with a loving spirit, turning any disappointments about preaching into petitions rather than criticisms.

Most important, familiarize yourself with the sermon by *meditating in private* upon what you have heard in public. Paul wrote to the Corinthians, "I declare unto you the gospel which I preached unto you, which also ye have received, and wherein ye stand; by which also ye are saved, if ye keep in memory what I preached unto you" (1 Cor. 15:1– 2). Meditation helps us digest truth and personalize it. One sermon properly meditated upon with the assistance of the Holy Spirit will do more good than weeks of unapplied sermons. Meditate upon each sermon as if it is the last you will hear, for that may well be the case. If additional private study on the text helps you meditate, by all means, take time to do it. Read commentaries on the text, such as those by John Calvin, Matthew Henry, Matthew Poole, and contemporary authors who soundly and ably expound the Scriptures. Finally, pray over the message and apply it to your life.

3. *Put the sermon into action.* A sermon is not over when the minister says "Amen." Rather that is when the true sermon begins. In an old Scottish story, a wife asked her husband if the sermon was done. "No," he replied, "It has been said, but it has yet to be done." Always seek to live out the sermons you hear, even if that means denying yourself, bearing your cross, or suffering for righteousness' sake. Lis-

tening to a sermon that does not reform your life will never save your soul.

James 1:22 – 25 tells us, "Be ye doers of the word, and not hearers only, deceiving your own selves. For if any be a hearer of the word, and not a doer, he is like unto a man beholding his natural face in a glass: for he beholdeth himself, and goeth his way, and straightway forgetteth what manner of man he was. But whoso looketh into the perfect law of liberty, and continueth therein, he being not a forgetful hearer, but a doer of the work, this man shall be blessed in his deed." Too many people listen to a sermon, see themselves in the mirror of the Word, and leave church convicted, but on Monday morning, they abandon all the truths they have heard. Of what value is a mind filled with knowledge when it is not matched with a fruitful life?

True listening means applying the Word of God. If you do not practice the Word of God after you have heard it, you have not truly listened to God's message. As seed that falls in good soil produces fruit, so the person who truly understands the Word produces fruit in his life.

Many people do not live out the truths they hear from the Word of God. Here are some reasons why that happens.

- They do not have saving faith. As 2 Thessalonians 3:2 says, "For all men have not faith." Some people oppose the gospel out of unbelief and rebellion, while others remain neither

hot nor cold. Still others who are too spiritually lazy to care, do not receive "the love of
the truth, that they might be saved" (2 Thess.
2:10). We must ask ourselves: Am I a real
Christian? Is it possible that I am making no
progress in practicing God's Word because I
have never been saved?

• They love sin too much. The author of Hebrews
speaks of the *pleasure* of sin. Often I hear
people say, "I know this is not right, but it is
just the way I do things." Or they excuse themselves, saying, "I just can't give it up," or, "I
could be doing something worse."

• They suppress what they hear. They smother
the God-given convictions that they hear and
quench the voice of conscience with carnality
and busyness.

• They focus more on the minister than on applying the sermon. These people often do more
church-hopping than Christian witnessing. The
advice John Newton gives is especially appro-
priate for such people:

  What I have observed of many, who run
  about unseasonably after new preachers, has
  reminded me of Proverbs 27:8, 'As a bird
  that wandereth from her nest, so is the man
  that wandereth from his place.' Such unset-
  tled hearers seldom thrive: they usually grow
  wise in their own conceits, have their heads
  filled with notions, acquire a dry, critical,
  and censorious spirit; and are more intent
  upon disputing who is the best preacher,

than upon obtaining benefit to themselves from what they hear. If you could find a man, indeed, who had a power in himself of dispensing a blessing to your soul, you might follow him from place to place; but as the blessing is in the Lord's hands, you will be more likely to receive it by waiting where his providence has placed you, and where he has met with you before.[4]

• They do not obey the voice of God. The first love of a Christian motivates zeal. But when that first love slips away, some believers begin to backslide. Many falter because they were never told how to obey the Word. They were never taught how to be loving, forgiving, and holy, or how to manifest the fruits of the Spirit (Gal. 5:22–23). Yet the Bible speaks much about obeying God, doing good, and not becoming weary in well-doing. In Romans 12, Paul instructs the church in Christian conduct. The Epistle of James offers wisdom in how to use the tongue, do good works, and follow the will of God.

How can we put into practice what God's Word commands us to do? Here are some guidelines for practicing the Christian life.

1. *Listen carefully to sermons that teach us how to live.* Like the Bereans, search the Scriptures to see

---

4. Newton, *Works*, 1:220–21. Cf. D. Martyn Lloyd-Jones, *Preaching and Preachers* (Grand Rapids: Zondervan, 1971), 153–54.

whether what you hear is truth. Listen with discern-
ment. When you are convinced that a message is
scriptural, ask yourself: How can I put this sermon
into practice? Perhaps you just heard a sermon on
the need to flee from certain sins. Ask yourself: How
can I shun the sins that have been pointed out? What
steps must I take to do that? Or perhaps you just
heard a sermon why Christians must speak to others
about Christ. You are a recent convert and have never
spoken to your father and mother about Christ. Ask
the Lord what to say, think about how to say it, then
pray for the opportunity to speak.

2. *Ask older, more experienced Christians for advice.*
Talk to people who are spiritually mature about how
to live as a Christian. For example, ask such a wise
person: What does it mean to love your enemies? Let
him explain what that means to him.

If after searching God's Word, consulting with
mature believers, and examining your own conscience and motives, you still do not know where
God is leading you, try stepping back. Ask yourself:
What is God's overarching commandment for all my
actions? Is it not that I am to love God above all and
my neighbor as myself (Matt. 22:37–39)? Realizing
that will move you away from love that springs from
self or the devil to love focused on God.

Loving God and our neighbor compel a life of service. People who truly love God serve God and their
neighbor, for that is how Christ lived on this earth.

Christ laid His glory aside that He might empty Himself and be a servant to His Father and to sinners (Phil. 2:6 – 8). Practicing the truths that we hear makes us more like Christ.

3. *Thank God for all that you receive from sermons.* Give glory to God when you are able to put God's instruction into practice. Often, I fear, we receive little because we are not grateful for what we receive. The Heidelberg Catechism states that "God will give His grace and Holy Spirit to those only, who with sincere desires continually ask them of Him, and are thankful for them" (Q. 116).[5]

4. *Lean upon the Holy Spirit.* Beg God to accompany His Word with the effectual blessing of the Holy Spirit (Acts 10:44). The preached Word will be a transforming power in our lives under the Spirit's blessing. If these directions are ignored, the preached Word will lead to our condemnation. As Thomas Watson wrote: "The word will be effectual one way or the other; if it does not make your hearts better, it will make your chains heavier."[6]

Jesus warns us in Luke 8:18, "Take heed therefore how ye hear: for whosoever hath, to him shall be given; and whosoever hath not, from him shall be

---

5. *Doctrinal Standards, Liturgy, and Church Order* (Grand Rapids: Reformation Heritage Books, 1999), 81.

6. Watson, *Body of Divinity*, 380.

taken even that which he seemeth to have." All of the means of grace will be taken away from inattentive hearers on Judgment Day. It will be too late for them to hear another sermon. The market of free grace will be closed forever, and the door of God's ark will be eternally shut.

On the other hand, if we have learned to be hearers and doers of God's Word, we will receive much in this life. One truth rightly received and practiced paves the way for more Christian truths. Eventually, practicing those truths brings believers into the fullness of Christ. They will grow in the grace and knowledge of Christ until they appear in Zion, filled with the fullness of God.

How may we know if the Spirit of God is applying the Word to us? We may know by what precedes, accompanies, and follows that application. Prior to the Spirit's application, He makes room in our souls for the Word. With the Spirit's application, we have a sense of rightness and power, whether it is the still, small voice of the gospel (1 Kings 19:12) or the thunder of Sinai (Exod. 19:16). That persuades us that we are receiving exactly what we need for our souls. Most importantly, when God applies His Word to our souls, "the fruits of righteousness, which are by Jesus Christ, unto the glory and praise of God" (Phil. 1:11), become evident in us. Our old nature is mortified and the sinful cult of self begins to decrease; our new nature is quickened and Christ's presence in our lives increases. If such evidence of the Spirit's work is lacking in us, we know that the Word is not being used profitably. "For the tree is known by his fruit," says Matthew 12:33b. These fruits include true conversion (Ps. 19:7a), wisdom (Ps. 19:7b), joy (Ps. 19:8a), peace (Ps. 85:8), sweetness (Ps. 119:103), freedom (John 8:31–32), praise (Ps. 119:171), and light for the dying (Ps. 19:8b).

Are you an active hearer of God's Word? Are you a doer of that Word? Or do you listen to sermons half-heartedly? If so, repent of your sin and begin to actively listen to His Word. It is not enough for you to attend church. You must be an active hearer and doer of the Word. Thomas Watson warns lukewarm listeners: "Dreadful is their case who go loaded with sermons to hell."[7]

If you have spent your entire life being a half-hearted listener, remember Jesus' parable of two sons whose father asked them to work in his vineyard. The first son said he would go, but when the time came, he did not go. The second son spurned his father, but repented afterward. He then returned to the vineyard and worked for his father. If you have not listened to the instruction of the Father, return to Him in repentance and humility. Seek His grace to hear, to obey, and to put into practice the Word of God.

"Take heed, therefore, how ye hear."

---

7. Ibid.

Attending Prayer Meetings

"These all continued with one accord in prayer and supplication, with the women, and Mary the mother of Jesus, and with his brethren."

— Acts 1:14

The Need for Prayer Meetings [5]

"We shall never see much change for the better in our churches in general till the prayer meeting occupies a higher place in the esteem of Christians." So wrote Charles Spurgeon in his famous address, "Only a Prayer Meeting."[1]

By "the prayer meeting" Spurgeon meant a formal meeting of members of a Christian congregation at stated times for the purpose of engaging in united prayer. Such meetings are the focus of this article; hence I use "corporate prayer" below as referring to these meetings in distinction from formal worship services.

Prayer meetings in America have fallen on hard times. Less than ten percent of members now meet for prayer in churches that once had vibrant, Spirit-led meetings. In many churches, prayer meetings have become cold and boring. Other churches have

---

1. *Only a Prayer-meeting* (Ross-shire: Christian Focus, 2000), 9.

never developed the tradition of meeting regularly for corporate prayer.

Lewis Thompson rightly wrote, "If it is true that the active piety of a church rises no higher than it manifests itself in the prayer-meeting, so that here, as on a barometer, all changes in spiritual life are faithfully recorded, then certainly too much attention cannot be given by both pastor and people to the conducting of the prayer-meeting."[2]

It is time to reassess the importance of prayer meetings, for the church that does not earnestly pray together cannot hope to experience reformation and revival. Have we forgotten that the Reformation era churches often held daily services for preaching and prayer? Is it surprising that the Reformed faith has experienced more revival in Korea than nearly anywhere else in the world in the last half-century when Christians there gather 365 mornings a year for prayer (at 5 a.m. in the summer and 6 a.m. in the winter)? Let us take a closer look at prayer meetings, specifically at their scriptural warrant, history, purposes, and implementation in regular congregational meetings. May God convict us that we have lost our first love concerning prayer and enlighten us to remember from where we have fallen, how we should repent, and how we may return to doing the first works (Rev. 2:4 – 5).

---

2. Lewis O. Thompson, *The Prayer-Meeting and Its Improvement* (Chicago: W. G. Holmes, 1878), 16.

The Biblical Warrant for Prayer Meetings

The warrant for corporate prayer is rooted in Scripture. In his book on the history of prayer meetings, J. B. Johnston asserts that corporate prayer is rooted in Genesis 4:26, where we read, "then began men to call upon the name of the Lord." Johnston writes, "Men, moved by grace, would then, as now, find enjoyment in social prayer, and would, consequently, be led by its power to practice it as now."[1]

The patriarchs also engaged in corporate prayer. Genesis 21:33 says that Abraham "planted a grove in Beersheba, and called there upon the name of the Lord, the everlasting God." That kind of group prayer in groves, often called "proseucha" (places of prayer distinct from sacrificial altars), continued throughout the patriarchal period, though later they were idolatrously abused (Deut. 16:21). David and his friends engaged in corporate prayer (Ps. 4:13, 14; 66:16), as

---

1. J. B. Johnston, *The Prayer-Meeting, and Its History, as Identified with the Life and Power of Godliness, and the Revival of Religion* (Pittsburgh: United Presbyterian Board, 1870), 27.

did devout Jews in Babylon (Ps. 137:1–2). In Nehemiah 9, at least eleven Levites took turns praying and confessing sin to the Lord before the children of Israel (vv. 4–5). Even the sailors who threw Jonah overboard first corporately call upon the name of Jehovah (Jon. 1:14).

Malachi 3:16–17 asserts the importance of meeting for spiritual fellowship, in which prayer very likely had a part: "Then they that feared the Lord spake often one to another: and the Lord hearkened, and heard it, and a book of remembrance was written before him for them that feared the Lord, and that thought upon his name." John Brown of Haddington concluded from this text that God was heartily pleased with corporate prayer; he said God "hearkens to, and hears, and honorably records, what is said; and esteems and spares the conscientious attenders."[2]

The New Testament continues to model corporate prayer. Services of prayer were held each morning in the synagogues of the Jews and in the Temple. More importantly, Jesus often led His disciples in corporate prayer, both before His death (Luke 9:18) and after His resurrection (John 20:19, 26). Gethsemane appears to have been one of Christ's favorite places to pray (John 18:1–2).

---

2. John Brown, "Divine Warrants, Advantages, Ends, and Rules, of Fellowship-meetings for Prayer and Spiritual Conference," in *Christian Journal; or, Common Incidents Spiritual Instructions* (London, 1765), second part, 18.

Jesus Himself provides an explicit mandate for prayer meetings in Matthew 18:19–20: "If two of you shall agree on earth as touching any thing that they shall ask, it shall be done for them of my Father which is in heaven. For where two or three are gathered together in my name, there am I in the midst of them." The Greek verb for "agree" that is used here is συμφωνέω (sumphōneō), which means "to sound together." This word is often used to depict the harmony of musical instruments sounding together, from which we derive the word "symphony." Jesus says that if you voice petitions together with fellow believers, He will do what they ask, providing it be in accord with His will (1 John 5:14). In a sermon titled "The Social Prayer-Meeting," preached in 1844, Edwin F. Hatfield of New York said that the Matthew text suggests that "any number of praying souls, two or more, have much greater reason to expect success when they pray together than when they pray for the same things separately."[3]

Peter Masters goes a step further, asserting that Matthew 18:19–20 is not only a promise given by Christ, but also an ordinance commanded by Christ. He writes, "When the Lord uttered these words, He was instructing the disciples about church affairs, particularly the procedure for dealing with misconduct in the church. He was not speaking to a casual hand-

---

3. "The Social Prayer-Meeting," in *The American National Preacher* 8, 18 (1844):171.

ful of believers, as though giving an optional prayer
opportunity to those who wished to meet informally
(although His promise certainly includes this). He
was giving official instructions to His churches. He
was inaugurating the duty of corporate prayer."[4]

The mandate for prayer meetings is particularly
reinforced in the book of Acts through the practice of
the New Testament church. Acts 1 and 2 show us that
the church prayer meeting, blessed by the Spirit, gave
birth to Pentecost. After Jesus' ascension to heaven,
the disciples continued earnestly in prayer until the
Spirit was poured out: "These all continued with one
accord in prayer and supplication, with the women,
and Mary the mother of Jesus, and with his brethren" (Acts 1:14). On Pentecost, 3,000 were converted
as a fruit of the disciples collectively voicing their
petitions and longings. After Pentecost, the disciples
continued steadfastly "in the apostles' doctrine and
fellowship, and in breaking of bread, and in prayers"
(2:42). When Satan afflicted the early church with
fierce persecution, the New Testament church met
corporately for prayer until the Lord heard their cries
and filled them with boldness to continue preaching
(4:24–31). Acts 4:24 says, "They lifted up their voice
to God with one accord." The Greek word used here
actually means "a concert of voices."

Persecution raged again, however. When James

---

4. *The Power of the Prayer Meeting* (London: Sword & Trowel,
1995), 19.

was beheaded and Peter imprisoned, believers once more sought God's guidance in prayer meetings. They prayed earnestly for eight days in several different locations right up to the hour that Peter was to be executed. The Lord then wondrously intervened by sending an angel to deliver the apostle (Acts 12:7). As soon as Peter was freed from prison, he went straight to the prayer meeting. Obviously, he knew where the believers would be gathered. The church, much like us today, could scarcely believe that God had answered their prayers and brought Peter back to them unharmed (v. 16).

When the church was spreading in Acts 13, certain prophets and teachers at Antioch, including Barnabas and other notable leaders, ministered, fasted, and prayed together. As they were so engaged, the Holy Ghost revealed that He wanted Barnabas and Saul to be separated for His mission work (vv. 1–2). Verse 3 says, "When they had fasted and prayed, and laid their hands on them, they sent them away." The Greek scholar A. T. Robinson asserts that the Greek actually speaks of "many upturned faces." The portrait painted here is one of numerous unitedly upturned faces, appealing to God in heaven. Paul would later acknowledge in 2 Corinthians 1:8–11 that the prayers of the saints was one of the most important reasons he was able to persevere in the ministry.

Acts 16 tells us how the first church in Europe was born in a women's prayer meeting as Lydia's heart opened to the gospel message (Acts 16:13–15).

Later, Paul and Silas held a midnight prayer meeting
in jail. As the disciples "prayed and sang praises unto
God," other prisoners were listening (Acts 16:25).
God responded to those prayers by sending an earth-
quake that set Paul and Silas free. The jailer and his
family were converted; the gospel triumphed, and the
church was comforted (vv. 26 – 40). God once more
affirmed His benediction on prayer meetings.

The New Testament epistles also commend
prayer meetings. Johnston says Ephesians 5:19 and
Colossians 3:16 probably refer to prayer meetings.
Though these texts are subject to various interpre-
tations, there are other examples of New Testament
churches in the epistles that appear to have engaged
in corporate prayer, such as the churches of Aquila,
Nymphas, and Philemon (1 Cor. 16:19; Col. 4:15;
Philemon 12). The epistles also encourage corporate
prayer by repeatedly using the second person plural
when calling believers to prayer (Eph. 6:18; Phil. 4:6;
Col. 4:2; 1 Thess. 5:17; 1 Tim. 2:1– 2; 1 Pet. 4:7).

The practice of the New Testament church shows
that prayer meetings should support the stated
assemblies for worship rather than compete with
them. They have an important but ancillary function
to the assembling of the church around the proclamation of the Scriptures.

The History of Prayer Meetings $\boxed{7}$

Prayer meetings have been a key part of evangelical Christianity throughout church history. They have not always been conducted in the same way, however; nor have they been called by the same name. Some prayer meetings have led to the formation of formal prayer societies or worldwide concerts of prayer.

Throughout the years, prayer meetings have been particularly influential in times of persecution and times of revival. During persecution, the church has often been forced to meet in private homes, both for corporate worship and corporate prayer. That was true of the ancient church in the catacombs as well as later groups such as the Waldenses, Lollards, Hussites, and Huguenots.[1]

During Reformation times, soldiers often held prayer meetings. Johnston comments, "These prayer-meetings among the soldiers of the armies of the Dutch Republic, as far back as the times of William

---

1. Johnston, *The Prayer-Meeting, and Its History*, 131–37.

the Silent, Prince of Orange, have much to do with the full tide of civil and religious liberty enjoyed by us today. Trace back American liberty—all that is noble and Christian in it—along whatever line of history we may, to English Puritans, to Holland or Scotch Presbyterians, we will find its cradle is the prayer-meeting."[2]

During the persecution by the Stuarts in Scotland, small groups met in prayer to help believers sustain faith and courage. They continued to meet until the Glorious Revolution of 1688; believers then continued to hold regular prayer meetings on weekdays in their homes. During that time, groups were often organized according to gender—men and women meeting separately. Often, pastors met by themselves. Some pastors led prayer sessions with the children of their congregations. Arthur Fawcett says there is abundant evidence that children's prayer meetings were often "run by the children themselves."[3] Children in these groups learned to publicly pray aloud without embarrassment. Later, many of these children became ministers or ruling elders in Christian churches.

Some prayer groups were formally organized by the Scottish Covenanters as "praying societies." These societies served the needs of the Covenanters when they had a paucity of ministers to organize

---

2. Ibid., 137.

3. Arthur Fawcett, *The Cambuslang Revival* (London: Banner of Truth Trust, 1971), 65–67.

their bonds as churches. Later, praying societies
became more systematic, often with strict membership requirements. In 1714, for example, Ebenezer
Erskine and sixteen other men signed a list of rules
for the praying society of Portmoak in Fife, Scotland.
Membership required coming to prayer meetings
at least twice a month. Three to six members of the
society prayed at each meeting. One question of
"practical divinity" was addressed each week, and
members voted on which question would be dis-
cussed the upcoming week. If a member missed two
or more consecutive meetings, he had to explain why.
After several unexcused absences, a member would
be asked to leave the society.[4]

Prayer meetings were popular in the seventeenth
century in certain areas of the Netherlands, especially among religious refugees. Fawcett tells of a
group of exiled ministers that met weekly for prayer.
At one gathering, the Puritan John Howe, known for
his great intercessory gifts, prayed with such fervor
that he broke into a great sweat. His wife crept up
behind him, took off his wig, dried his sweat with her
handkerchief, then reset his wig, all while he continued praying. About that same time, James Hog, later
of Carnock, writes that when he studied at one of the
Dutch universities, he met with many who formed

---

4. Donald Fraser, *The Life and Diary of the Reverend Ebenezer
Erskine* (Edinburgh: William Oliphant, 1831), 523–26.

religious societies and "poured out their hearts unto the Lord in prayer with one accord."[5]

Prayer meetings were especially influential in times of revival. The 1620s revival in Ireland was spurred on by prayer meetings.[6] So were awakenings in the 1740s. Two generations prior, Josiah Woodward had published *An Account of the Rise and Progress of the Religious Societies in the City of London,* which described forty distinct prayer groups in London.[7] As the awakenings spread, prayer meetings multiplied. Thomas Houston writes in his *The Fellowship Prayer Meeting,* "The awakenings which took place in various parts of England, under the ministry of Wesley and Whitefield, led to the establishment of social prayer-meetings; and, at this period, when *within* the pale of the National Establishment, and *without* it, all was under the torpor of spiritual death, this organization was a powerful means of exciting earnest minds to pursue after eternal concerns."[8]

Prayer meetings were also influential in eighteenth-century revivals in Scotland. Prior to the awakening in 1742, numerous prayer societies had

---

5. Fawcett, *The Cambuslang Revival,* 58–59.

6. *The Prayer-Meeting, and Its History,* 110, 145; cf. Thomas Houston, *The Fellowship Prayer-Meeting,* 80–84.

7. Cf. F. W. B. Bullock, *Voluntary Religious Societies, 1520–1799* (London, 1963).

8. Cited in Johnston, *The Prayer-Meeting, and Its History,* 154.

sprung up. One society was established in Kilsyth in 1721; it flourished for some years, then died out in the 1730s, but was resurrected in 1742 just before revival broke out. During the meetings, there were public prayers, psalm-singing, Scripture reading, and discussion based on questions from Thomas Vincent's study of the Shorter Catechism.[9]

During the Great Awakening in Scotland, prayer meetings often began with children, then spread to adults. For example, a schoolteacher in the parish of Baldernock allowed four students to meet on their own for prayer and psalm singing. According to *The Parish of Baldernock*, "In the course of two weeks, ten or twelve more [children] were awakened and under deep convictions. Some of these were not more than eight or nine years of age, and others twelve or thirteen. And so much were they engrossed with the one thing needful as to meet thrice a day—in the morning, at mid-day, and at night." Adults then began holding prayer meetings two or more times a week. There were many conversions at both the adult and the children's meetings.

The fervor soon spread to other parishes. *The Parish of Kirkintillock* reports: "In the month of April, 1742, about sixteen children in the town were observed to meet together in a barn for prayer. Mr. Burnside [their pastor] heard of it, had frequent meetings with them, and they continued to improve.

---

9. Fawcett, *The Cambuslang Revival*, 71–72.

And this being reported, many more were impressed. Soon after, about a hundred and twenty [children] were under a more than ordinary concern, and praying societies, as usual, were formed."

Johnston's reaction to that awakening was to affirm and support the prayers of children. "Why not encourage children's prayer-meetings? Why may not God still perfect praises to the glory of his grace, out of the mouth of babes?" he asked.[10]

Jonathan Edwards also encouraged children's prayer. In answering objections some critics had raised to children's prayer meetings, he wrote, "God, in this work, has shown a remarkable regard to little children; never was there such a glorious work amongst persons in their childhood, as has been of late in New England. He has been pleased, in a wonderful manner, to perfect praise out of the mouths of babes and sucklings; and many of them have more of that knowledge and wisdom that please him, and render their religious worship acceptable, than many of the great and learned men of the world. I have seen many happy effects of children's religious meetings; and God has seemed often remarkably to own them in their meetings, and really descended from heaven to be amongst them. I have known several probable instances of children being converted at such meetings."[11]

---

10. Johnston, *The Prayer-Meeting, and Its History*, 165–66.
11. Cited by ibid., 173.

In 1747, Edwards published *An Humble Attempt to promote an explicit agreement and visible union of God's people through the world, in extraordinary prayer, for the revival of religion and the advancement of Christ's kingdom on earth.* Usually referred to thereafter as *An Humble Attempt*, this book was reprinted by Christian Focus in 2003 as *A Call to United, Extraordinary Prayer.* Edwards said he was motivated to write on "a concert of prayer" for two reasons: first, he realized that the revivals of the mid-1730s and the early 1740s would not recur until God's people engaged in earnest prayer for revival. Second, he wanted to provide additional theological support for a document written by some Scottish pastors simply entitled *Memorial.*

David Bryant tells us the story of *Memorial*: "Rising out of scores of prayer societies already functioning in Scotland around 1740, especially among young people, by 1744 a committee of ministers determined it was time to do more. They decided to try a two-year 'experiment,' uniting all prayer groups and praying Christians in their nation into a common prayer strategy. They called for focused revival prayer on every Saturday evening and Sunday morning, as well as on the first Tuesday of each quarter. By 1746 they were so gratified by the impact of their experiment that they composed a call to prayer to the church worldwide, especially in the colonies

(*Memorial*). However, this time the 'concert of prayer' was to be for seven years."[12]

Citing Zechariah 8:20 – 22, Edwards said that God's rich promises encourage us to expect great success from corporate prayer, especially world-wide concerts of prayer.[13] He said: "That which God abundantly makes the subject of his *promises*, God's people should abundantly make the subject of their *prayers*." He concluded that when believers persevere in united concerts of prayer around the world, God will grant a fresh revival, which "shall be propagated, till the awakening reaches those that are in the high-est stations, and till whole nations be awakened."[14]

Edwards's book had a limited influence during his lifetime. Republished late in the eighteenth century in England, it influenced William Carey (1761–1834) and his prayer group. It also affected John Sutclif (1752 –1814), a well-known Baptist pastor in Olney, who led weekly prayer meetings for revival in the Baptist churches of the Northamptonshire Asso-ciation, to which his church belonged. Those prayer meetings spread throughout the British Isles, particu-larly impacting eighteenth century revivals in Wales.

12. Jonathan Edwards, *A Call to United, Extraordinary Prayer* (Ross-shire: Christian Focus, 2003), 16 –17.

13. See Edward Charles Lyrene, Jr., "The Role of Prayer in American Revival Movements, 1740 –1860" (Ph.D. dissertation, Southern Baptist Theological Seminary, 1985), 31– 81, for a helpful study of Edwards on the concert of prayer.

14. Edwards, *A Call to United, Extraordinary Prayer*, 18.

Heman Humphrey writes in his *Revival Sketches*, "One of the most important revivals of religion, when the effects are considered, is that which occurred in the 'Principality of Wales' under Howell Harris and Daniel Rowlands; and this was carried forward and fostered by means of private societies for prayer and religious conference."[15] In the end, tens of thousands were converted throughout Britain from the 1790s to the 1840s.[16]

Edwards's treatise became a major manifesto for the Second Great Awakening in America in the late 1790s. It was reprinted in 1794 by David Austin, and later that year, after discussing the book, a group of New England ministers meeting at Lebanon, Connecticut, decided to promote a renewed concert of prayer according to the original Scottish plan as set forth in Edwards's treatise. Twenty-three of these ministers signed a circular letter that was sent "to the ministers and churches of every Christian denomination in the United States." After prayer was held successfully in many different denominations, other circular letters and concerts of prayer followed.[17]

Through the three-decade Second Great Awakening, corporate prayer was widely accepted as God's

---

15. *Revival Sketches and Manual* (New York: American Tract Society, 1859), 55ff.

16. Erroll Hulse, *Give Him No Rest: A call to prayer for revival* (Durham: Evangelical Press, 1991), 78–79.

17. Lyrene, "Prayer in American Revival Movements," 97–100.

primary key to open the door to revival. Leaders of
the day, such as Nathanael Emmons (1745–1840)
and Timothy Dwight (1752–1817), taught that there
was an indissoluble link between God's purposes
and prayer. Not that prayer could change God's purposes, but, as Dwight wrote, prayer is "the means of
procuring blessings, for without prayer the blessings
would never be obtained."[18] Not surprisingly, therefore, there were numerous movements for prayer,
both at the congregational level and in larger, organized concerts of prayer in geographical areas. These
movements typically stressed praying for the outpouring of the Holy Spirit for their personal lives,
their families, their churches, and the human race.
In turn, these congregational prayer meetings and
concerts of prayer gave impetus to the establishing of
numerous mission societies that strove courageously
to bring the gospel to the unchurched in America
and to the heathen around the globe. For example,
the first decade of the nineteenth-century alone saw
the establishment of the New Hampshire Missionary
Society (1801), the Missionary Society of Hampshire
County in Massachusetts (1801), the Missionary
Society of Rhode Island (1801), the Piscataqua Missionary Society (1803), the Maine Missionary Society
(1807), the Vermont Missionary Society (1807), as

---

18. Timothy Dwight, *Theology Explained and Defended,*
4:127.

well as scores of other missionary societies organized by various denominational bodies.[19]

Edwards's treatise also fueled other awakenings in the late 1850s. Samuel Prime's *The Power of Prayer*, published by Banner of Truth Trust, explains how corporate prayer ushered in the famous 1857–1859 revival (sometimes called the Third Great Awakening) along the eastern coast of the United States, then spread west, resulting in the conversion of hundreds of thousands of people.

Beginning in the fall of 1857, six men gathered at noon every day for corporate prayer in the consistory room of a Reformed church in New York City. Prayer was the Spirit's means to germinate the seeds of revival. By early 1858 more than twenty prayer groups were meeting at noon in New York City. In Chicago, more than 2,000 people gathered daily for prayer at the Metropolitan Theatre. The movement spread to nearly all the major cities of America, then made its way to the British Isles and around the world. Prayer meetings sprang up everywhere: in churches, on college campuses, in hospitals, among sailors, on mission fields, and at orphanages and colleges. To mention only one example, at Hampden-

19. Lyrene, "Prayer in American Revival Movements," 102–136; Oliver Wendell Elsbree, *The Rise of the Missionary Spirit in America: 1790–1815* (Williamsport, Pa.: Williamsport Printing and Binding, 1928), 47–83; Charles L. Chaney, *The Birth of Missions in America* (South Pasadena, Calif.: William Carey Library, 1976), 154–79.

Sydney College, one student found another student reading Joseph Alleine's *Alarm to the Unconverted*, and told him that there were two other students who were also in favor of such literature. The four students held a prayer meeting, while fellow students harassed them. When the president heard that the four young men were accused of holding a prayer meeting, he said with tears, "God has come near to us," and joined them himself at their next meeting. A remarkable revival swept through the college and into the surrounding area. Soon, more than half the college was attending prayer meetings.[20] Scholars estimate that two million or more were converted in the revivals of the late 1850s, while hundreds of thousands of professed Christians were deeply affected.[21]

In the 1860s, Charles Spurgeon organized prayer meetings at the Metropolitan Tabernacle. People met at 7 a.m. and 7:30 p.m. every day. More than 3,000 came to the meeting on Monday evenings. One evening a visitor asked Spurgeon what accounted for the success of these meetings. Spurgeon walked his visitor to the sanctuary, opened the door, and let him watch the participants. Nothing more needed to be said.

The great revivals of the twentieth century were likewise inspired by prayer. The Welsh revival of 1904–05, the revival in Riga, Latvia, in 1934, and

---

20. Johnston, *The Prayer-Meeting, and Its History*, 185–87.

21. Cf. Lyrene, "Prayer in American Revival Movements," 187–218.

more recent revivals in Romania and Korea were all born and nurtured in prayer.[22] Today, most evangelical churches hold weekly prayer meetings, but there seems to be so much lukewarmness in prayer. We desperately need churches to unite in the kind of prayer that the Spirit may use to produce world-wide revival.

Our National Prayer Day is a step in the right direction, but much more is needed. Believers need to pray earnestly all around the world in new concerts of prayer for God's Spirit to bring worldwide spiritual awakening. Let us pray wholeheartedly with John Sutcliffe, "O for thousands upon thousands, divided into small bands in their respective cities, towns, villages, all met at the same time, and in pursuit of one end, offering up their united prayers, like so many ascending clouds of incense before the Most High! May He shower down blessings on all the scattered tribes of Zion!"[23]

---

22. Hulse, *Give Him No Rest*, 103–7.

23. David Austin, *The Millennium* (Elizabeth Town, N.J.: Shepard Kollock, 1794), iv.

The Purposes of Prayer Meetings 8

According to John Brown of Haddington, prayer and fellowship meetings serve the following purposes:

1. To promote and increase the knowledge of the truths, ordinances, and works of God (Col. 3:16; Ps. 111:2).

2. To express and exercise mutual sympathy among the members (Rom. 15:1–2; Gal. 6:2).

3. To provoke and encourage one another to holiness and virtue, in all manner of conversation (Heb. 10:24–25; Eph. 4:15–16).

4. To communicate one another's gifts and graces to mutual edification (1 Pet. 4:10; Eph. 4:12–13).

5. To render [members to be] faithful and friendly watchers, counselors, and reprovers of one another (1 Thess. 5:14; Heb. 3:13; 10:24).

6. That [the members] may join together in

prayer, praise, and other spiritual exercises (Matt. 18:19 – 20).[1]

Brown's list summarizes the scriptural foundation of prayer meetings. There are additional purposes for prayer meetings:

7. Praying together is often the means God uses to initiate or increase revival.

8. Praying together increases the commitment of believers to the kingdom of Jesus Christ at home, throughout the nation, and around the world.

9. Praying together provides an important spiritual oasis in a busy week. R. J. George writes, "It comes midway between the Sabbaths to arrest the rushing tide of worldliness, and to draw the Christian apart from the exacting cares of this earthly life; and it makes him "'to sit in the heavenly places with Christ.'"[2] Prayer meetings cultivate a tender, devotional spirit, as well as quiet, inner strength in the midst of trials.[3]

10. Praying together increases unity in the church. As Johnston says, at prayer meetings, "unity has its birth-place; here it is cradled; here it

---

1. Brown, *Christian Journal*, 18 –19.

2. R. J. George, *Lectures in Pastoral Theology, Second Series: Pastor and People* (New York: Christian Nation, 1914), 30.

3. Thompson, *The Prayer-Meeting and Its Improvement*, 19, 27.

is trained; here it becomes a three-fold cord; here is the centre of the unity of the church; for here is the soil—the genial soil beside the waters—where unity strikes deeply its roots, and whence it draws its life-power to bind together in comely brotherhood."[4]

Peter Masters puts it this way: "In the prayer gathering, preoccupation with ourselves as individual believers slips away, and we become a group of people longing for the blessing of others, and for the prosperity of the cause. In the prayer gathering we are refined and honed as a united body of people. It cements unions, and promotes respect. We hear each other pray; we subordinate ourselves to each other; we appreciate each other. We feel, as the old saying goes, one another's spirits, and we are warmed and deepened in oneness and regard. To adopt a well-worn phrase, the church that prays together, stays together."[5]

11. Praying together utilizes the spiritual life of the church for the good of all the church's ministries. When members are called to exercise their Spirit-empowered gifts in prayer, the spiritual power generated from the prayer meeting pervades all of the other ministries of the church. Thus, the prayer meeting serves

---

4. Johnston, *The Prayer-Meeting, and Its History*, 77.

5. *The Power of Prayer Meetings*, 15–16.

as an important connecting link between the Spirit's power and human instrumentality.[6]

12. Praying together increases the Christ-centeredness of believers. David Bryant writes, "Prayerfulness is the natural response of a heart that is fully caught up in all Christ is to us and for us, over us and within us, through us and before us and upon us. Christ defines our agenda in prayer. Christ opens up the door to heaven to present our prayers. Christ gives us unity in himself even as we pray. Christ is the ultimate answer to all our prayers. In other words, prayer and the supremacy of Christ must forever walk together."[7]

13. Praying together provides an education in prayer for the entire church. Believers grow in the gift of prayer as they hear others pray. They learn to appreciate specificity in prayer, passionate pleading, Christ-centered wrestling, and fresh modes of expression. Iron sharpens iron. Young believers learn from older ones, and older believers are encouraged by the sincere petitions of the younger.[8]

14. Praying together enhances private prayer. It makes us realize that, due to the intercessions of Christ and true believers, every time

---

6. George, *Lectures in Pastoral Theology, Second Series: Pastor and People*, 30–31.

7. Edwards, *A Call to United, Extraordinary Prayer*, 24.

8. Masters, *The Power of the Prayer Meeting*, 16.

we pray, we are entering a twenty-four hour per day prayer meeting. Surely this ought to increase our expectation and fervency as we pray in "private."

15. Praying together demonstrates our complete dependence upon God's sovereign power and gracious blessing for all His ministries and all our work in His church and kingdom. It is a corporate recognition that without Christ we can do nothing and that with Him we have large expectations. Praying together helps us turn our eyes heavenward to the God of the harvest who has promised great things. It focuses our minds on large-scale blessings.[9]

---

9. Ibid., 15.

Implementing Prayer Meetings 9

Here is a suggested order and time schedule for a congregational prayer meeting:

• *7:30 –7:45 Opening by leader*
  A consistory-appointed leader opens the meeting with the singing of a fitting psalm, a short Scripture reading, and a short meditation packed with succinct, heart-warming truth, designed to awaken the lethargic and to edify the spiritually hungry. George advises, "Aim to have the remarks practical, experimental, and devotional, rather than doctrinal or controversial."[1] The entire opening, including the meditation, should not exceed fifteen minutes. The leader should normally speak the meditation in his own words, though he may on occasion choose to read some edifying comments by a biblical author.

---

1. George, *Lectures in Pastoral Theology, Second Series: Pastor and People*, 39.

• *7:45 – 7:50 Gathering of prayer requests*

For the next five minutes, the leader collects prayer requests (both verbal and written). These should focus on the glory of God and the coming of His kingdom. They may include prayers for the needs of church individuals and families, specific churches, one's denomination, the nation, evangelistic endeavors, or a church ministry. The leader then reads the list and encourages people to pray without lengthy pauses and with sufficient volume so others can hear.[2] Private or trivial prayer requests should be avoided at a public gathering. Nothing can dampen a prayer meeting so quickly as long pauses, inaudible prayers, and trivial requests.

• *7:50 – 8:25 Prayer by the members*

People should be reminded that all prayer needs the blessing of the Holy Spirit. Prayer should be offered in the right spirit: humble repentance, humble confession, humble petition, humble earnestness, and humble praise. And all prayer should be uttered in the name of Jesus Christ, outside of whom no prayer is truly answered.

• *8:25 – 8:30 Closing prayer and doxology*

After about an hour, the pastor or leader should close with prayer. If the period of silence after a given prayer becomes excessively long, the leader may

---

2. Spurgeon, *Only a Prayer-meeting*, 20.

choose to end the meeting a bit sooner. The meeting
could conclude with the singing of another psalm or
doxology.

Suggested rules and practical guidelines

1. The consistory (or session or board) should
    supervise the gatherings and select the person
    who shall lead the opening devotion for each
    meeting. A subcommittee could be appointed
    to implement the prayer meetings, but the
    consistory should retain the final word.

2. The consistory should provide church mem-
    bers with guidelines for prayer meetings.
    Those guidelines should include a short
    list of the purposes of prayer meetings. The
    document should encourage the entire con-
    gregation—including children—to attend
    these prayer meetings.

3. The consistory should stress that only pro-
    fessing members of the congregation may
    lead the gatherings and pray aloud at them.
    That will prevent problems that could arise if
    visitors pray without knowing the guidelines
    of the meetings.

4. The location, time, and other specifics of
    prayer meetings should be clear. These
    details should be printed in the bulletin. The
    pastor should pray for them regularly from
    the pulpit, emphasizing their importance to

the congregation. He should regularly and warmly encourage the entire flock to attend these meetings, elevating them above every other church activity and ministry. These meetings could be held in various places in the church, providing the acoustics are good and the seats are comfortable. If a microphone is used, people should be told how close it should be held to the mouth.

5. People should have a humble and affectionate manner towards each other throughout the meeting. That means avoiding issues, questions, or controversial expressions in prayer, as well as terms that are difficult for the average member to understand. Prayer time should not be used to preach or explain doctrine or correct someone. A prayer meeting is not the place to debate or argue. Prayer meetings are only edifying when they focus on common prayer needs.

6. People should pray for things great and small. They should pray for the glory of God, the growth of His people, the conversion of sinners, and worldwide revival. They should pray for their ministers and missionaries and theological students to be anointed by the Holy Spirit, for their office-bearers to be faithful, for the church to live in unity and peace, and for every church ministry and outreach

to flourish and bear fruit a hundredfold. They should pray for the elderly, the lonely, the sick, and the youth. They should pray for troubled marriages, broken families, and prodigal sons and daughters. They should pray for governmental leaders, for the forsaking of national sins such as abortion and Sabbath-breaking, and for a return of biblical truth and morality in the land. But they should also pray for smaller, personal prayer requests, focusing on one or two of them—preferably those that have not yet been addressed—so that their prayers, as a general rule, do not exceed five minutes. Those who are prayed for should be mentioned by name. Their specific needs should be addressed, much as Paul did in Romans 16 and in other epistles.[3]

7. People in a congregation have various gifts. At a prayer meeting, they should remember that God doesn't value prayer according to how eloquent or skillful they are, but rather, according to the heart. No person should be reproved for halting or stumbling in prayer. Rather, we ought to bear with each other's weaknesses.

8. People ought to pray privately prior to these

---

3. Erroll Hulse, "A Lively and Edifying Prayer Meeting," *Reformation Today*, no. 95 (Jan–Feb 1987):22.

meetings for the blessing of the Holy Spirit. They ought to ask God for the blessing of Spirit-wrought, Scripture-based revival. As Spurgeon said, "Let us not waver through unbelief, or we shall pray in vain. The Lord saith to his church, 'Open thy mouth, wide, and I will fill it....' We want a revival of old-fashioned doctrine, a revival of personal godliness, a revival of domestic religion, a revival of vigorous consecrated strength."[4]

4. Spurgeon, *Only a Prayer-meeting*, 9.

The Importance of Prayer Meetings

10

Erroll Hulse writes,

You can tell with a fair degree of accuracy what the church is like by the demeanor or substance of the weekly prayer meeting. Is there genuine evangelistic concern? If so, it will be expressed in the prayers. Is there a heartfelt longing for the conversion of unconverted family members? If so, that is sure to surface. Is there a world vision and a fervent desire for revival and the glory of our Redeemer among the nations of the world? Such a burden cannot be suppressed. Is there a heart agony about famine and war and the need for the gospel of peace among the suffering multitudes of mankind? The church prayer meeting will answer that question. Intercession in the prayer meeting will soon reveal a loving church that cares for those who are oppressed and weighed down with trials and burdens. Those bearing trials too painful or personal to be described in public will nevertheless find comfort in the prayer meeting, for there the Holy Spirit is especially at work.[1]

Edwin Hatfield concluded his sermon on prayer meetings by saying that those who conscientiously and habitually participate in them usually "experience more sweet and pure delight in [their] very exercise," "grow more rapidly and steadily in grace," "become the most devotional, active and useful Christians," and "become the life and soul, as it were, of the Church."[2] What about you? Is that not what you want to be?

Do you support your church's prayer meetings with secret prayer and with your presence? Have you grasped their purposes and value? Do you agree with Matthew Henry who said, "When God designs mercy, He stirs up prayer"? Do you believe that God is sovereignly pleased to tie together revival and prayer? Do you understand that the success of your minister and missionaries is intimately bound up with your prayers?

Do you realize the value of attending the prayer meeting together as a family—the value of teaching your children verbally and by example that just as your own family is bonded together by pray-

---

1. "The Vital Place of the Prayer Meeting" (Pensacola, Fla.: Chapel Library, n.d.), tract-3, opening page.

2. "The Social Prayer-Meeting," in *The American National Preacher* 8, 18 (1844):177–80.

ing together, so the church family grows and stays together by praying together? Teach your children that besides the actual worship services on Sunday, no church activity is so important as the congregational prayer meeting. Train them to know that true Christians — not politicians or the worldly powers that be — hold the key to the future of the family, the church, and the nation through the instrumentality of private and corporate prayer.

If every God-fearing family in every God-honoring church around the world took the congregational prayer meeting seriously, what impact would that have around the globe? If God agrees to do what two or three ask in accord with His will, what will He do if thousands and millions ask in accord with His will? I believe that Scripture and church history teaches us that the future of our children, our family, our church, and our nations depends on God's people storming the mercy seat together. Prayer is the normal means that God uses to shower His heavenly blessings upon the earth.

If your minister were to announce that at your forthcoming prayer meeting, the apostle Paul would appear, the entire congregation would attend. That, of course, will not happen, but something more important will: the Lord Jesus Christ will be there. He is the silent and yet speaking guest at every prayer meeting where two or more are gathered in His Name. He promises not to miss one. He will hear every lisping prayer. He takes them all to heart.

We customarily record our appointments on our calendar. Will you not mark your church prayer meetings on your calendar as engagements of the highest priority for your entire family? Will you not prepare for them, and try to bring a friend or two with you?

In *Hints and Thoughts for Christians*, the nineteenth-century pastor John Todd wrote two chapters titled, "How to Make Our Prayer Meetings Dull" and "How to Make Our Prayer Meeting Interesting." To make a prayer session dull, he, in effect, suggests: "Suppose the meeting is tonight. Don't pray about it today. Try to find some excuse for staying away. Are you not very tired? Aren't you coming down with a cold? If you do go, arrive late. Feel no responsibility to pray. If you do pray, see how long you can be. The world is full of things that need prayer. Bring them all in. Or else, use your prayer time to scold those who are present. Then, after the meeting, criticize in the presence of your family those who prayed."[3]

Making the meeting interesting takes more work. Here's a summary of what Todd suggests, "Let the prayer meeting live in your heart. Consider a Scripture or a thought or two that can be profitably offered up in prayer. Pray for the meeting in your family worship. Pray that Christ will be manifested in the meeting. Pray that the Holy Spirit may be present to warm, cheer, and animate every heart. Feel responsible for

---

3. Cf. Phil Arthur, "How to Spoil a Prayer Meeting," *Evangelical Times*, Sept. 2005, p.15.

it. Make it a solemn duty, a habit, and a privilege to be there. Above all, pray at the meeting. Participate. Let your prayer be short and diverse. Don't harp on one string. Avoid praying for that which has already been mentioned. Be hopeful and expectant; believe Christ when He promises to be in the midst of even two or three gathered in His name."[4]

Dear friends, let us treasure prayer meetings. Let us engage in them with all our heart, remembering that revivals usually begin with prayer meetings. As one divine put it, "The Holy Spirit loves to answer petitions that are appended with many signatures."

Let us keep praying. Let us pray without ceasing. God is able to do "exceedingly abundantly above all that we ask or think" (Eph. 3:20). Who can tell what He will do?

---

4. *Hints and Thoughts for Christians* (New York: American Tract Society, 1867), 99–110.

SCRIPTURE INDEX